Martyrs of a Certain Belief

Poems by

Anthony Desmond

Martyrs of a Certain Belief

ISBN-13: 978-1-7345158-4-8

Cover image is a derivation of the following work:

"Prometeo con lo specchio e l'aquila" by Francesco Maffei used
under Creative Commons CC BY 1.0 {{PD-1923}}

Printed in the U.S.A.

For more titles and inquiries, please visit:

www.thirtywestph.com

Table of Contents

Pride

Fragile as an egg,
the yolk of man bursts
sunny side up in the
darkest room, his shell
so empty, yet illuminated
by the bulb of sinners,
shaded like a lamp to dull
the damage they've done.

Lasso

Even my fantasies
are bound by the rules of reality.
But I don't care because
I can't touch you in real life.
So the fact that you're in
arm's reach like the
moon in my daydreams is oddly satisfying—
though I can't feel at all.

Martyrs of a Certain Belief

Son

I'm ashamed of the fact that my
third eye illuminates only
when I'm dragged by the neck
through a cemetery of fools,
knowing I belong in one of the graves.
My face is unfamiliar, yet recognizable,
as a stranger, I once knew in a past life.

Myths of a doppelganger's
death sentence opened my mind
like clogged pores because
I'm my father's twin, yet my father
is a piece of shit, so I often question why
I bear resemblance to dung
that fertilizes the earth; thus, I am here
for reasons beyond me. I help others grow
and collect rings like a tree in the deepest forest.

I am a cave where the waters are hidden
and untouched by devils' hands.
I crave to satisfy my thirst, but my tongue
mimics the horn atop the head
of ignorance where the price of beauty
hangs like a semi-hard cock, riddled with flaws.
Still welcomed by every mouth willing to swallow
a shot of glory, like time, doesn't exist
and vanity is set in stone.

The Last Poem

I threw my favorite shoes in the lake; the lake was no more than about four feet deep, so I could still see them if I ever chose to come back. I walked towards a fork in the road. I picked whichever way the sun's blinding rays were shining. I ran every breath a hope for endless pots of gold. I stumbled upon a cactus. I put my hands on it. I jammed my hands into it like an angry man putting holes in thin apartment walls. I bled; the sting lasted for hours. I kept the laces from those now-watered-down shoes—I needed them to make a noose. Sweat dripped into my eyes, still no match for the sting of prick-filled hands. The salty taste on my tongue was of my mother. Sweat reminded me of home. I was a man, a strong man, with too much to carry. I wanted to be that carefree boy again, but that was impossible, like knowing the exact moment of a stranger's death. I finally came to an old tree—thick, bare, and deathly haunting; the branches were sturdy enough to string up my every hope and all my dreams. Stripped bark across the bottom revealed a gathering of bees. The Queen was in the center. I assumed she was happy. The only queen that would ever give me comfort was not a human being, but a bee—nothing but a fucking bee. I was home, but still, I was worthless. I climbed the tree, took my shirt off, baked in the blistering heat. As time told me what I needed to do, a single gust of cool air ran across my entire body. I closed my eyes, shut off all my senses. As soon as I awoke, I felt a hot road and small bits of rock cutting the skin between my toes. I knew what I had to do: I buried the noose and went back to the lake.

Why I Am Afraid to Look in the Crystal Ball

I looked the devil in the eye
while on the verge of becoming a king
and saw ancient mathematics
in hieroglyphs and petroglyphs of
the Kama Sutra. He welcomed me with great
zeal and handed me a crown soaked
in Jesus' blood with added fats to make
it more attractive. My belly forked with
hunger. It was a road designed to crumble;
thus, I persisted in writing
my wrongs in a book of death that
glowed red like holding a flashlight
to your mouth.

I became obsessed with entitlement
and anything that wasn't mine, wasn't worthy.
No one touched my hands—
no man, no healer,
no woman, no fortune teller. I couldn't
stop thinking of that dance with Satan,
yet I didn't feel a goddamn thing.
Darkness did a number, and I stood still,
as if it was life or death.
That same blood was now dry, and
I sank my teeth like a dream warning
of a loved one's demise.
Nubs and trigger-shaped wisdom
pulled like a baby's grip, and I left
with a familiar pain.

Disclosure

Let me tell my story—
feel free to glorify the horrors when I'm gone.
Because I would die for this.
It's kill or be killed, and I am the lucky one
in this world of primogeniture
with self-inflicted wounds on my wrists.

I can't handle the pressure—
so everything I'm too afraid to do,
I'll layer it in metaphor
and hope you'll understand that
my intentions were good,
despite my hatred
for the amiable disposition.

Downpour

I wish late nights with my memories
were a sanctuary of milk baths.
but as I approach the last sip,
the bottom of the bottle
sits like a tub overflowing
with madness, making me wet
like pussy lips after great sex,
because of these shallow waters.

Sometimes I gather the nerve
to step out and fake friendships
with people, although I'm paranoid that
everyone has a knife behind their back.

Other times I stand there,
my clothes soaked as if I walked
through New Orleans during
Hurricane Katrina, yet
the only thing I've been swimming in
is the disappointment of my loved ones
that folds over their faces
like the moon in the calmest river.

Balance

I wish to crawl into a paradise
of lucid dreams where I can hear you
calling my name while I sleep,
because these memories are like
the kickback of a shotgun
that's knocking too close to my heart.

I watch the devil dance when I awaken,
so, I close my eyes to hear your voice
against the taiko drums of a god
that silence the doldrums of my reality.

My Only Friend

The pull of a trigger
accompanied by an empty barrel
can be just as soul-crushing
as the blood dripping from my ear
that's commonly mistaken
for a lipstick print on my collar,
as if I'm having a good time
with loose friends
like the lips of a loquacious
beauty that's too good to be true.
I cling to loneliness
like static to laundry,
like a man desperately
pursuing an unreachable love
but can't afford the
travel costs. I crave life,
yet I'm so satisfied by
the climax of death
that living just leaves me
wanting more.

Ultramarine (Violet)

Drawing blood for tigers
And diving in the stream
Leaving the scent of violet

Grinding pigmentation
Down to ultramarine
Proving synthetic
As the grey film
Over your eyes

Naturally amaurotic
To magnanimity
As Medusa
Feeling the weight
Of strobe lights
Falling from grace

Ultramarine (Blue)

A feast of deities
With wolves

The honey of your
Omnipotence

The viscosity
Of felsic magma

Weakness

Flood me like a lone streetlight amid
the darkness, and in deep thoughts of
you, I'll swim for the heavens like a
stroke of genius as I lie on my back and
let you create the masterpiece; the
artist remains anonymous—like a
nightmare with the bride wearing a veil
she's too afraid to lift. I am a canvas
covered in a tarp, and you **refuse**
to take a look at what you helped
create, because you hate
the stench of truth like the scent of
paint. A face too like your own,
you wish the hardness of this angel
could turn you into stone. And still you
are the weight that I wasn't ready to
handle; thus, I am a broken levee, and
my tears are the water that turned the U.S.
citizens to refugees—foreign feelings in
a native heart.

I Understood

He said,
"Nobody could read such a tragedy
and dare to smile!"

"Well, I guess I'm just a dysfunctional bastard.
That's what seeing the evils of pain will get you."

After so much heartache,
you learn to find joy.
I've heard some disgusting tales
that'll probably lead someone
to believe I'm heartless.
I've gained immunity from it.
the power over me is no more.

Like pulling out my teeth
and pretending to bleed
the blood of Christ
as I spit it out.

After leaning on affliction for so long,
I learned to stand alone.
They said independence is forever—
until you fall in love.
Then your weaknesses
become their strengths.

Like never hearing of religion
and worship the word of the wild
out of the underlying fear
that reincarnation doesn't exist.

Ram's Head

Devil horns on the head of a black sheep.
Blood of an orange, visceral as a
puckered asshole in heat.
Reducing myself to metaphor, though
these words can't bleed for me.

Lashes on my back from poetry that crawls
underneath my skin, as God pulls these
broken stanzas from the depths
of my being which I am forced to re-read
and relive: a moment foolishly captured
by the gift given to those who don't ask for it.

Saltwater ink,
only visible to the
mind's eye drips
from the horns of
the black sheep
with no choice but
to admire the
yolk of the sun,
the shell of the moon,
all the bursts and
all of the cracks
in loving someone
who can't love me back?

Little Truths

"That's life," they always say.
I realize I'm a broken record,
telling you things you don't
care to hear. Break me in half,
though I never divide equally
like a wishbone, and still
they won't come true.

A slap on the wood
to rid the dust off its heart.
Spiked trees—two pricks, like
a snake's fangs injected
the sap, like the venom bite
of a tongue, piercing as
lies glaze like honey.

The Holy Ghostwriter

If these words could uplift themselves
off the page, they would praise you
like a pastor on his knees.
As you bathe me in these metaphors—
like the soap that drips off your curves
and drops into the water,
like a nightcrawler to a largemouth bass—
you bait me without saying a word.
For now, we're both mutes, and our
bodies form a bond that has its own
language only we can understand.

Rosewater Baptism

I deaden these feelings
like oxygen to the wine.
Still, the subtle aroma
of you pulls me with
the strength of
a hungry hand
gathering fruit
off the vine.

To Drift Amidst the Raging Tide

There is a bomb in everyone,
waiting to exit like the final days—
and you know this is coming.
When the lights are off, the fuse shines.
And as it shortens, our frustrations
grow taller like the sixth foot of everyone's desire.
Regardless, I don't regret those days
I spent doing nothing; that's when I saw
God at the feet of the one
I wished to praise.

Conditions

The best of the best
are often the
best of the worst—
like a saber tooth
under a gold cap.
like glass blown into
the shape of a diamond.
If it doesn't cut the mirror,
you ain't worth a dime,
but like a high-class whore
in broad daylight,
you shine,
sweetie.

Landscapes

The fluidity of night
runs smooth like a train
on brand new tracks.
I dream of riding
that train, of one
of the cars being my home—
complete with
a mail-order bride.

A rare find—like
a white boot with
no scuff marks—
and the curves
on her body
match the
dramatics of her
heavy German accent.

Symbolism

A priest will burn her
And her hair will
Blow in the wind
And into the faces
Of everyone
Who is without sin?
Like God picking wheat
Only to leave
Empty-handed

Sadist || Masochist

Smoke in the air
acts as a deity—
the part of me
that's undoubtedly grotesque,
yet amazingly endearing.
I feel myself growing old,
though I still find pleasure,
like a cigarette in a hailstorm.
By the time it fills my lungs,
I'll be ready to die the death
we fear—
that is the God
we believe in.

The Good Ole Days

I'm a dreamer of plain songs
and the simplest imagery
of an owl perching
on a bust with a face
too close to mine—
deja vu of when
disapproval defined
the lines that ran across
my forehead.

Swallow

Lost in the essence of a still night,
memories of you consumed me like flies
around the cantaloupe rind,
and I'm in the midst of this swarm,
looking for a bite of flesh
that might have been overlooked.

The scratch in my throat
was a heart aching
to be worn on my sleeve
like a pair of cufflinks,
and the other was out there
waiting to be found.
Still, I'll save this just for you.

Flower

The cold steel in my mouth
is reminiscent of you.
Swallowing feels like
a knife held against
my tongue, and
I am a masochist
with my hands full
of precious belongings.

My belladonna:
you never know when
to stop pouring yourself
all over me; this love is
like rose water except
you're overpowered
with a taste that keeps me
coming back for more,
and I keep falling for
the nightshade that
dilates your pupils.

Take a Hint

I'm slowly backtracking
to that point in my life
when I lost faith in
everything. The Cross more so
resembles a whore with her
legs open rather than
Jesus waiting for a hug. I feel like
everyone is against me;
and I'll sleep off these
thoughts until their banging
on the headboard awakens me.
You've been quiet lately,
so I'll be a mute like a mime
crying out for help
but nobody cares enough
to pay attention—just drop a dime
and keep walking.

I pour my heart out to you,
but you refuse to be a vessel
for my tears or my love.
Still, I thought you'd have no choice
but to fill your cup if I kept
pouring my soul into your ears.
Now I'm alone in the wet sands
of sorrow, mourning as it deepens.

Sweet Cream

Lonely lovers caw—
like vultures
over a dead body,
picking at the flesh
of a no-good nigga—
and wonder why their
stomachs churn
like a farmer's wife.

Beholder

Such hatred of the sun
has become the apple
of my eye—
like a comely woman
with features well alive
in the dead of winter,
freezing her ass off for me.
I must let my guard down,
so, her figure becomes moot,
and I, baking like a
delicate souffle,
am ready to sink
with any disturbance
as little as the removal
of her shoes
after a long day.

Bark

The texture of a cork tree
is a deformity among mankind—
one who's incapable of
gaining love from another,
like the stillness of nature,
roots planted in the bile of
a leper with fascination,
like a baby's discovery
of their limbs.

I Never Told You

Like the thrill of making the unknown tangible,
I believed I'd break the curse
of the good dying young.
Well, I won't be known for my ingenuity,
but please tell someone
to remember my intellect and wit,
even if they don't know who I am,
like I wish I knew myself.
I'm trying to remember the people
I once loved so much,
yet I don't know their names,
let alone their faces—
like being ashamed of the fact
that I'm colorblind, and my lover
is threatening me
while covering his eyes.
I couldn't see such tiny details
that meant the world—
the only gateway to
such a beautiful soul.

I never told you.

Cock

The tease of a dead-end
without a forewarning
fissures like an asshole
that belongs to a lover
with ulterior motives.
The walls can't speak,
but crack under pressure—
like God showing you a sign.
A chandelier could hang
on the guilt like a suicide
victim and swing until
the last flinch. It lingers
like a soul out of body
on judgment day, as heaven
is dependent on whether
or not you're a martyr
for your belief.

Lungs

Sands of relevancy
deplete like an hourglass,
and I'm at the bottom
waiting for you.
As these moments fill my lungs,
I choose not to breathe
in my efforts to hold on
to something that was never
mine to lose.

Palms

I draw maps and go to war.
I feel so comfortable with
my hand on the trigger
(with my hand on you).
With my hands, I hold
blame and guilt;
with my hands, I hold
greed with a grip
tighter than a deadly sin—
though there ain't a dime
in my pocket.
So is that a contradiction,
or is everything I'm
holding onto just pretend?
These hands hold secrets,
and the security of
insecurities line my palms
like loyalty in
the fangs of a snake.
These hands love you
more than I should,
but these hands also
hate you.

They hate you
because I dug and dug
and scooped
the dirt of your affection;
I held it like a thirsty child
desperately trying not
to let one drop hit the ground.
They hate you because
I was mistaken. These hands
fooled me; these hands
carried loneliness and held
it above my head.

The Deaf

I burned the skin off my fingertips
to numb my existence
and further, leave no traces—
aside from these words in print—
because I'm tired of talking
to those who hear me but
always fail to listen.
Cut off my tongue and
serve it on a platter
while maids pour drinks
like the 1960s.
Dissect my brain like a frog
for the whole class to see.
But these thoughts are
only audible to hearts
that can catch a beat
like the cracking of a whip
against a slave's back
for wanting to be heard.

Resting

I found a home in solace, and now
I'm afraid my love for being alone
will one day turn into a pool
of loneliness that I'll have
no choice but to drown in,
like a ghost in the summer,
starving for a vessel
to drift atop these waters.

Nightly Rituals || Morning Affirmations

I often ask myself
how to kill this piece of my conscience
that's taking my every ambition
and set me up for failure
before I even get out of bed.
I tell myself I'm handsome while
wishing a Kvartil chandelier could
follow me around the stores
people like me can't afford to be in.

I say in the mirror, "You're intelligent,"
but still, find me dumbfounded
by the curvature of ancient pyramids
and how they sculpted god-like faces
without the use of modern technology.

I'm left in the dark,
and the answer is in all the numbers
tattooed in bold black ink against my skin,
so it's impossible to do the mathematics.
Not even the fear-induced braille going
down my arms can help me figure out
why we are the way we are...
I'll just plant indigenous seeds in ivory soil
and watch a flower sprout and die
from the refusal of food and water
because it doesn't recognize its beauty.

The Forsaken

Lonesome as the hunter
and the hunted,
both afraid of nudity—
the prey is thyself,
bothersome as the saliva
of her father dripping
from the snake's fangs.
And while the lonely
women make friends
with soft-shell crabs,
they see such fine delicacies
forsaken in their rawest form.
Shades of blue fade at the
tips of their claws, like the
mascára that now barely
lines her eyes.
As it seeps into the corners
of her mouth, she palavers on
like the soft-shell crab's
last steps through mud and
into the waters that dictate
the flow of her tears but doesn't
hold the thickness of her father's saliva.

She follows the tide
with the smell of sex in her hair.

Holding On

In the evenings when the sun looks like
an apocalypse is when you feel the most.
Shadows in the night hover, even existing
when the light flickers; they've traveled
with the stars, we run from and to,
like a loved one with a firm embrace.
We've outgrown nurturing arms—
until they become a handful of memories.
Only then do we trace the ends
of our hair instead of cutting them.

Holes

Cork your transparency like
a wine bottle; I am air, and once
you've exposed such vulnerability,
things won't ever be the same.
My porousness is your modern-day
convenience. I can test
the waters alone as your presence
lingers like the aroma of cherry pie,
but the scent alone won't satisfy
my hunger.

Armor

Whilst drowning in the light of others,
I held out a bowl with hopes of satisfying
my hunger for love.
Each spoonful lead me to realize
that I was the heir to hatred,
because what filled that bowl
had such an acquired taste.
As it seeped through the hole
in my heart,
I stood in a piss puddle
of regret,
barefoot and salty
like cries during sex,
because loving someone
out of loneliness
is like suddenly finding God
at the moment when
your life flashes before you.
There is no belief,
just selfish fear,
like shielding yourself
from a bullet with a child
and destroying the purity
of first love.

Naivety

I'm a sensitive human being:
my feelings are like a flash
override to a motherboard with
too much information to process.
So what more do you want from me?
Whatever you can take—like a thief
in an empty house, yet I
trust you enough to leave
my home with empty hands.

Bible on My Sleeve

Deceived by these walls
and the lies they tell me,
verses bled through the cracks
that I had no choice
but to believe in as they echoed
like prayer through
a megaphone,
churching me with fear.

Faith

The fluidity of your presence
let my love runneth over
like the Holy Grail
with teachings my heart
no longer believed in.

Maybe I'm Selfish

I momentarily live with the satisfaction
of knowing who I am, until the rug
gets pulled from under my feet,
like a failed attempt to pull a
tablecloth from under a place setting.
I pick up the pieces, and as I clean, the
hot food that once held the shape
of my world now sinks into the carpet
and leaves burn marks on my fingertips
which never quite heal because
I'm constantly tapping my middle and index
against my temple to clear my conscience.

When you realize you love the memory
of who that person was more than who
they are today:

I hate you
I love you   I hate you
I love you   I hate you
I love you   I hate you
I love you.

I wish you would change because
I don't like who you are, but I can't live in the past,
so it's become needing only the memories
until I can watch them fade away.

Life Jacket

I walk a constant sway on eggshells,
hoping I don't crack like the ones under
my feet. Anxiety can feel like the softest
nudge from death; it is a weight like a
laundry basket of apples instead of dirty
clothes, forbidden like said fruit.
I keep telling myself I don't deserve
a bite in the practice of shaming
entitlement, but I'm too familiar with
the feeling of never-ending desire.
Love and shame coincide with a plunge
in the deepest part of your chest,
and often I wish I couldn't feel
my body when I what I should wish for
is numbness in my heart.
What's fucked up is that I'm aware of everything
that's been said—
delusions of grandeur in reverse—
but people in power don't tell the truth.
We're made to believe that weakness
is a buoy tied to our salvation.
And one person's pain is a painting
that so many can relate to.

Body Snatcher

I wish I was morbid enough to love you to death,
but instead, I'll wait until death do us part.
May it be after a night of fucking
like we're not in love and I never
have to close my eyes again,
because being with you is like a dream,
and I want to feel alive until death do us part.

Like the strange fruit of my Adam's apple
on the Eve of your tongue, the devil in my eyes
tells you I only want one thing
as if we're not in love—the gap
between your legs, hollow
as your body to a pathologist.
I wish I was morbid enough to love you to death,
but I can only bear the thought of you
as my cadaver.

If I Shall Succumb to My Skepticism

I constantly tug on my earlobes to feel alive,
hoping to open another path—
to discover a new part of me.
The stretch never healed,
and the rawness of pain with
every spin of a marble teardrop
is like the sadomasochism of a saint.
I'm a monk performing
the sign of the cross with bodily fluids
on my fingertips, and the devil is waiting
in a pool of his saliva.

Unfortunately, I never learned how to swim,
so I awoke before I took that dive,
after I swallowed the apple.

I thought about paralyzing my sins
at the cost of my soul,
or a life filled with riches,
knowing I'll go to hell
while watching the clock wind down.
And with my final breath,
I'll kill my affinity for atheism
and be forgiven by way
of conversation
with Egyptian gods.

Silent Songs

You harbor my greatest fear
and my every passion.
You're all the soul
I could muster into this
shell of the man you helped me
become. Singing silent
songs of love amidst
the hard times and
daily struggles, like
flippin' nickels and dimes
into riches only made
for us.

Trusting

There is a stagger in my benevolence
because I'm ungrateful for the gift of
patience. Fake smiles wait like a
know-it-all to tell me how I feel
on the inside: Hurt. Anxious. Confused.
Sun-bathed without a lick of SPF—my
ancestors told me niggas don't need it.
There's a lot of things I didn't feel were
necessary, but skepticisms change,
and now I question the very things I see
instead of supreme beings and the
entities of pharaohs. I'll never know
what they wanted from me, but I have a
concept: we are not genius, bulging
muscle, nor the words rolling off our
tongues that we hardly believe ourselves.

Shade

Attack me like a lioness
with belladonna in her eyes.
Whatever is said,
let it be a metaphor for lust,
no matter how vehement
or melancholy.
Seduction acts as a psychedelic drug
and dilates your pupils
at the first glance of my cock.

The last sight you'll ever see—
like shooting eggs with guns,
the sun is a yolk busted by
deadly nightshade,
and it hardens over my teeth.
I kept my mouth shut
as you cried mascara tears that
soaked into the carpet
like rain over a city built
on the graves of holocaust survivors,
where the acidity and greenhouse gasses
are a constant reminder for the souls
that isn't resting in peace.

Sioux

I laid with you as an elegant nude,
accepting every hour
as another eccentricity,
in a bath of your lemon curd,
a climax of euphoria
from your full lips
down to the fat of your hips,
counting thy blessings as
one torn rib of man.
We create a cannibal's cave in the sheets
while two tongues wilt like dying roses
in an eclipse of atmosphere reminiscent of 3 a.m.
You light a cigarette while I play the flute
for this starless night as the face
of a hungry child graces the television set—
actors paid to enslave beggars
for a petty flashing light
encircled in smoke rings.
I still breathe fullness as pure
as my once-virgin tongue
now weaving between your teeth
as you slowly capture me in your jaw
for pleasures unknown,
plotting revenge like a sadistic fiend.
I am a cross at the scene of a tragedy,
overshadowed by tall blades of grass—
a venomous hold, sharp like
the structure of your face,
cheekbones giving me lacerations
along my spine with intentions to please.

Birdbath

Tonight I lie in fear
of losing you
while thoughts of
having you will
always stay in my head
and swell my tear ducts
like a water balloon.

I burst—
and down my face runs
a stream that mimics
the pouring of water
from an angel's fountain.
My hands are cupped
to pool the tears
I want so badly for
you to wipe away.

Straitjackets

Pellets on the floor,
scattered like seeds in the sand.
A shadow manifests in dawn's light.
A silhouette in shotgun shells mimics
God's figure out of silver, not bronze,
like the lies that get us through each day
we're meant to play our roles.

Call me a showoff, like a man
dressed in all white—a subtle target.
May the process that got me here
be my premonition,
except the silhouette would be
the most hated figure of myself.
May creativity fuel my critiques
while I pace back and forth
on this bed of cork crumbs
like the inside of a padded room.

A sane stupor homogenized—
even all my angels and demons
are draped in Italian leather.

Rugs

Mismatched necessities line
my fingers as I clasp them
like a gold locket which holds
a piece of my heart.
I talk to God only when I need to;
thus, these prayers
are sacred as fruit to a market
vendor birthed from the grounds
deserving of our praise.

6

An eloquent gypsy girl
With eyes of Medusa
Sculpted by the weight of ancestry
Chipping away at the only
Known picture of beauty

Spawning such blessings
As a free shower from a man
Washing his hair
Out the highest window

Caryatid with the skin of a leper
And thighs of a woman
Full as a squatting lover
Of butterfat turned modern

Martyrs of a Certain Belief

Make incisions until your past life
bleeds onto the floor
shallow enough to create a half-moon
using the arch of your foot,
which is the closest thing
to the view of a night sky
with the passing of each day.

The cuts on your arm start to resemble
Arab scriptures no one is allowed to read,
giving you the voice of a mime
doubling as a street preacher
on Hollywood Boulevard.

Idea of You

If only you cared to know,
I would tell you all the right things.
But you don't believe in yourself
because you lived through your
parents' mistakes instead
of making your own.
So the last thing you want to
believe are the words coming
out of my mouth, which you refer
to as "bullshit;" little do you know,
these words will fertilize you
like a seed, and every drop of your
saliva from the tip of my tongue
that enters your temple
will water your grounds like
a moat to protect you
from danger.

A Man and His Ignorance

He said,
"Playing on a white piano
is like touching my guardian angel."

I said,
"If they even exist;
they wouldn't waste a lifetime
watching over ungrateful pigs."

He said,
"Have you ever felt ivory keys
as smooth as a dove's back?"

I said, "I've never felt anything."

Unmarked Graves

I feel powerless when I look at you
sometimes. My impatience makes
me wonder if God exists or
if it's just Mother Nature in disguise.
Nonetheless, I see your true feelings
stream amongst the crocodile tears,
the fake bird calls, the killdeer bodies
that float to attention from the cesspool
of bullshit, the bloodlines cover-up—
six feet deep, holding secrets that drag
like a cement block around their ankles
going even further below the surface. Still,
I feel powerless when I look at you
sometimes. My impatience makes
me wonder if God exists or
if it's just Mother Nature in disguise.

Sheep

The backbone of my family
snapped like a twig,
and I got the shortest end—
hence why I don't believe in wishes.
I never got to make one
since I hated the blood
I saw surrounding my pupils
like rose-colored glasses
that wasn't fashioned for my face.
The blood-stained me enough
to become a hypochondriac,
so cutting my wrists
was out of the question.

I spend my life
sweeping broken glass;
these fragments of my face
line the floor,
become a kaleidoscope,
but like a bull, I was blind
to the colors. Still, I ran towards
my fears as if they were painted red,
but never quite got the kill shot.

Soap

I believe the words
these walls echo
when God speaks
in sign language.

Love is as immortal
as the essence of a mother
no matter how many times
it has drifted away like buckets
in a river where everyone
washes their hair.

Shades of You

I wanted you
to swim in the warm
blood of me,
but your cold shoulder
acted as a raft to
save you from what
you thought were
dangerous waters.
I constantly watch
you drift back to
the time when I thought
I knew you, and
I can't seem to find peace
now that the idea of you
is dead, like a widow
who refuses to shed a tear,
as if holding everything in
forms a stream for you
to come back to me.

Possible Effects of the Prelude

I am human enough to believe in the skeptics.
I believe in the ignorance of it, as well.
Human enough to remind me that
I am ignorant with confidence,
acknowledging you, yourself,
and I.

The antithesis of intellect is lust for
either hyper/objectum sexual craze
or the soul of a necrophiliac,
acknowledging you, yourself,
and I.

Lèse-majesté

The tension in my breath
holds like oils that form blackheads.
In this sanctuary of acid rain,
vilify my name so I may become
a god-like figure behind
ivory caryatids of royalty.
Replace the crowns with halos
to mimic guardian angels
at their lowest point.

I Am the Omega

The Alpha passes
without mourning, like a wolf.
Blood filters the air
as I leave a trail with my footprints.
Mortality is no apex,
but a transcendence within the red mist,
solidified like a shelter in the arms
of a loved one.

The Ritual

There are times when the homogeneous
seems the most attractive,
like a row of paper dolls
handled by your flesh, but the blood
that drips from the papercuts on my hands
ends up in this elixir
of turmoil and sibling rivalry.

By the stains on my fingertips,
one would assume I touched the needle
that so desperately holds this family together,
though I swear I never tried to sew a stitch.
Even after I wash my hands,
the water is just as thin
as what supposedly runs through my veins.
The towel soaks in my misery
and rubs off on the next person,
like a dirty sponge
reused over and over again.

Sacrifice My Sanity

These eyes are heavy
like a weight on the chest,
as if you fell across
my lap and slept
on transparency
while my legs grew numb
like a heart that's endured
too much pain. But I want
you to stay; the tingles don't
matter, nor does sleep.
Let my belly be your
scapegoat for hunger.
If only my dust
could salt your tears.

Everything I Wanted to Hear

My dominant wingspan
was made for you;
with promises of being
my eyes, you dragged me
down like fresh butter
being weighed on the
petals of a flower so
the bees couldn't rest
after gathering nectar.

When Everything Real is Gone

My admiration of porn is diminishing;
I've no more hope left
in the things in life that aren't real.
The hell inside others
no longer shines brighter than
the flames that burn these
tired eyes, causing my pupils
to char like love letters in a house fire.
Though my memories hold every word
he wrote to me, I'd still fall
into the burnt paper and rub it against
my skin just to feel some remnants
of warmth, but it'll never compare
to the inhalant that was his breath.

Love overlaps my mind
like shuffling cards,
while my vices hold me
tighter than the hug I gave
my mom after her hospital stay,
and my wingspan is the only
thing that stops these walls
from closing completely.

The Anomaly

"Why the fuck should I think for myself,
when you seem to grimace at the thought of me?
Might as well share my pain,
thus, share my world—
bring some light to this rain.
An artist rarely dies a peaceful death,
and I'm a happy drunk who's drinking quicksand
from the hourglass that is my bottle."

Those words are the start of my day. A tad cliché,
 but a shitty barely thought out poem
  is much easier to remember than Bukowski, cummings, Kafka...
   on days when alcohol takes me to bed
  and only a few more shots can get me out.
In a drunken slur, I'll attempt to thank God for this
  hangover by getting on my knees and leaning over my bed
   which reeks of whiskey
  reminding me to never (say never) drink again.
I don't speak to God aloud because I believe silence
  is my truest blessing. Sometimes I throw up in the morning;
    if I'm in the middle of a prayer,
   I keep my mouth shut and let it ooze through my teeth.

As I utter words in my head,
I wonder if this is what death
may taste like.
I wonder if this sickening, spoiled-milk-like
taste will be the last coating
on my tongue before I die.

It's ironic, because in my heart
I know I'm going to hell,
but that's why I believe—
it takes away the sting of
feeling like I'm already dancing
on the devil's feet.

Even at my worst, I think I can hear him talking back to me
(either that or the voices in my head):
the voice that tells you not to be afraid of death
   because that millisecond of pain
    when you put the gun to your head is worth the life you live;
the voice that tells you to reward yourself
   with shit that takes you two steps back.

I swear the most dangerous place a man can be
   is within himself.

Most prominent childhood specifics:

I go back to the times when my father used to cut my hair—he would take hours
  as he precisely trimmed it, as if I were his muse, though those were
   the times when I almost felt like a hallowed mannequin.

Instead of dismembering me from the waist down, my torso
    put on display for whatever occasion, I'd feel the scissors run
    across my ear after my dad specifically told me
    to be still.
I cried, swore up and down that I hadn't budged, and he'd cantankerously
    express his sorrows and finish my haircut in silence.

I distance myself from the life I wanted and the hearts
    I didn't mean to break.
From the perspective of a bystander,
    it shouldn't be too difficult to see how fear pushes you away
    from everything and everyone you love.
Blood aged like fine wine was dumped on me from the highest branch
    of our family tree which spawned a pair of strong hands.
    I recognized those hands by the protruding veins and hair
    slightly covering the knuckles.
Such a caress should be forbidden—the touch harnessed
    the power to turn a small child into a curmudgeon by the age of nine.
During adolescence, I saw how the blood of a family can run so thin,
    that if you put deep red dye in water the resemblance is uncanny.
You don't realize these things until you're too old to change.

I wish I could go back to the times when I stood tall and lean,
    admired the whites of my eyes and a face that was at least
    somewhat confident.
Now I can barely stand a glance at this naturally emotionless
    mug that houses the bitter hazes that were the windows to my soul.

Shadow Boxing

I shaved my entire body
in search of spiritual growth,
and now I miss pulling hair
out of my mouth.
Maybe a strand will fall
from heaven and wrap itself
around my spoon—force me
to take the bad with the good,
like being fed my last meal inside
a pillory. I'd rather chase what
haunts me than walk with someone
who's sure to stay by my side,
fuck someone who's disgusted by me
rather than make love to the one
who claims to be my soulmate;
thus, I'm left with nothing
in pursuit of everything
that isn't meant for me,
but this is all I've ever known
and the only thing I know
how to fight for.

Donor

That night, for the first time in my life, I just wanted
to go to sleep, and I didn't look forward to waking up.
I've had dreams of looking for you; in them, I was
a tree in the middle of the forest—no one heard me
fall, so no one would try to count my exposed rings
and piece together what happened. My body isn't
a cemetery and my heart isn't six feet deep;
I've no place to bury my demons, so they continue
to lay sod on the grounds of my faith.

I Hold You on My Back
For Frank Stanford

I have memories of moments
that never existed and
discussions that changed
my perspective, though I've
never heard your voice,
like I laid for eternity
watching you rest in peace
while your hair continued
to grow across my lap—
these divine entities
playing me for a fool.
I shaved my head
so the dead may epistolize
as my old hair mimics
the feather atop their pens.

Acknowledgments

The author wishes to thank the following journal in which some of these poems originally appeared

"The Last Poem," "6," and "A Man and his Ignorance" *Signal from Static* anthology (Chromatopia, LLC.)